I0799099

Snow

by Samuel Tipton
illustrated by Alan Kundera

Practice Pre-Decodable 10

McGraw Hill Education

Bothell, WA • Chicago, IL • Columbus, OH • New York, NY

MHEonline.com

Copyright © 2015 McGraw-Hill Education

All rights reserved. No part of this publication may be reproduced or distributed in any form or by any means, or stored in a database or retrieval system, without the prior written consent of McGraw-Hill Education, including, but not limited to, network storage or transmission, or broadcast for distance learning.

Send all inquiries to:
McGraw-Hill Education
8787 Orion Place
Columbus, OH 43240

ISBN: 978-0-02-140452-0
MHID: 0-02-140452-6

Printed in China.

8 9 10 11 12 DSS 27 26 25 24 23

See the 

.

See the  .

snow pants

See the  .

coat

See the 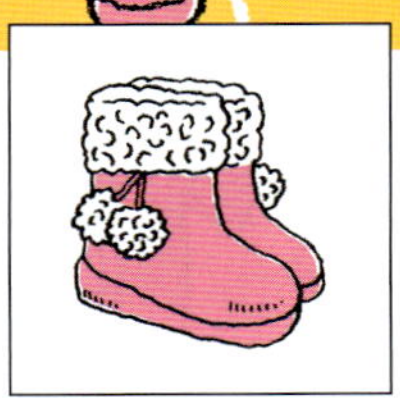 and .

boots

mittens

See the  and .

hat

scarf

See the  ?

girl